BEST AUSTRALIAN POLITICAL CARTOONS 2017

Russ Radcliffe created the annual *Best Australian Political Cartoons* series in 2003. His other books include: *Man of Steel: a cartoon history of the Howard Years* in 2007; *Dirt Files: a decade of Australian Political Cartoons* in 2013; and *My Brilliant Career: Malcolm Turnbull, a political life in cartoons* in 2016.

Russ has edited collections from some of Australia's finest political cartoonists, including Matt Golding, Judy Horacek, Bill Leak, Alan Moir, Bruce Petty, and John Spooner, and curated exhibitions, including *Moments of Truth*, *Dirt Files*, and *Suppositories of Wisdom*. In 2013, Russ was awarded the Australian Cartoonists Association's Jim Russell Award for his contribution to Australian cartooning.

for Jossie

BEST AUSTRALIAN
POLITICAL CARTOONS
2017

edited by
Russ Radcliffe

SCRIBE
Melbourne • London

Scribe Publications
18–20 Edward St, Brunswick, Victoria 3056, Australia
2 John St, Clerkenwell, London, WC1N 2ES, United Kingdom

Published by Scribe 2017

Cover, front: Mark Knight, *Herald Sun*
Cover, back: Andrew Dyson, *The Age*

Printed and bound in Australia by OPUS Group

Scribe Publications is committed to the sustainable use of natural resources and the use of paper products made responsibly from those resources.

ISBN 9781925322286 (pbk.)

A CiP record for this title is available from the National Library of Australia.

scribepublications.com.au
scribepublications.co.uk

Commissioned
and produced by

www.highhorse.com.au
russ@highhorse.com.au

Cartoonists

Eric Löbbecke, *The Australian*

Introduction

Reg Lynch, *The Sun-Herald*

Tell me it ain't so, thinks David Rowe's Liberty as she wakes with a look of wide-eyed terror the morning after the night before (p. 5). Yes, he was mouthy, a bit creepy, outrageously macho, but surely too clownish and preposterous to be really threatening? But how the hell did she end up going home with him?

Like many in the United States, Malcolm Turnbull must have felt a bit like the violated Liberty after that first getting-to-know-you phone call (p. 15) with Donald Trump. The straight-shooting president was getting ready to put all those free-loading minor powers in their place – from now on, relationships would be transactional. Forget business as usual.

And Australia's first transaction centred on our need to solve an unpleasant domestic political problem – the running sore of offshore detention camps (p. 18). Turnbull's promise that we will 'be there again and again' – the true price tag undisclosed – filled Pryor with dread, his supplicant PM returning from New York clutching the refugee swap deal like an appeasing Neville Chamberlain fresh from Munich (p. 21).

Anticipating the significance of any year – especially while we're so close to it – is probably foolish. Nevertheless, 2017 does seem like a global historical pivot, probably as significant as the fall of the Berlin Wall.

With the rise of the alt-right and the election of a Breitbart president hell bent on demolishing any residual notion that the US is the indispensable nation or the light on anyone else's the hill, the post-Cold War neo-liberal global consensus underwritten by the US seems all over bar the shouting (p. 136).

How do we know? Because Donald and his éminence grise Steve Bannon have told us so (p. 56). America First means the reconfiguration of the US role as one self-interested player among many – albeit with the biggest guns. As Trump reminds us: 'Do you think we were so innocent?' At bottom it was probably always thus, but America was always able to convince itself of its own virtuous exceptionalism – even if it was illuminated by the red glare of ever larger rockets.

Sean Leahy, *The Courier Mail*

The establishment globalists around the administration may prevail over Steve Bannon's insurgent nationalists for a time, but the challenge

Andrew Dyson, *The Age*

to the Pax Americana, already well underway with the meteoric rise of China, has been given a mighty shove into a new world of multi-polarity and great power rivalry. Moir isn't too hopeful that cool heads will prevail as the world runs screaming to the bomb shelters (p. 54).

Everything around the president seems extravagant and parodic, and this is especially true of the escalating mutual threats between Trump and Kim Jong-un. When a man with his hands on the nuclear codes turns nuclear deterrence into a pissing contest between macho narcissists (p. 164) rather than a diplomatic problem to be carefully managed, it is no suprise that even a great cartoonist like Dyson might find his own satirical armoury somewhat blunted. Of course, Trump's tactic of 'the crazy-unpredictable' psychopath in his dealings with China and North Korea is straight out of Richard Nixon's Vietnam-era playbook (p. 68). With Nixon, it was clearly tactical calculation; with Trump, it's hard to avoid the impression that his twitter feed is plugged directly into his id.

It wasn't long into the administration that other comparisons with Tricky Dick were being drawn (p. 158). The sacking of James Comey over the 'Russia thing' (p. 60) invited memories of the removal of special prosecutor Archibald Cox in 1973, and talk of impeachment gathered pace.

But Trump is a deeper expression of a broken system that has created enormous wealth for some but ripped the heart out of communities across the US. Removing him will neither solve those social and political failings, nor the electoral problems of the Republicans or Democrats.

The economic nationalists on the alt-right claiming to stand for the little (white) guy provide a powerful and, for some, an attractive counterpoint to the establishment. The consensus on what is to be done, or even what now constitutes the common good, has broken down: whatever happens next, it's too late to return to politics as usual. As we have seen in Charlottesville, all kinds of grotesqueries and atavisms — white supremacists, the KKK, neo-Nazis, anti-Semites — have emerged from the political fissures which now run at crazy angles across traditional loyalties and party lines (p. 167).

The conflict between a resurgent nationalism and cosmopolitanism is a global phenomenon, though the storms are not quite as uncompromising in Australia. Yet. But we do have our very own disruptor-in-chief, Tony Abbott (p. 24). Like Trump, his skill set is more

Cathy Wilcox, *The Sun-Herald*

Mark Knight, *Herald Sun*

suited to insurrection than governance, and has been applied ever more single-mindedly to bringing about Malcolm's downfall in an increasingly overt campaign. And we have our very own 'deplorables' committed to holding the line for a narrow nativism (p. 26).

Peter Dutton's attack on Malcolm Fraser's immigration policies was at the pointy end of an otherwise platitudinous discussion about values and Australian citizenship. Golding and Moir (p. 42) illustrate the ease with which this topic flips over into barely disguised racial dog-whistling that can only undermine our delicate racial harmony.

But it was the battle of manifestos (p. 142) that laid bare the very real ideological struggle between Turnbull's progressive small 'l' liberalism and Abbott's conservatism – battlelines potentially more threatening to the party's future than all the sound and fury of personal animosity and revenge-seeking. While both men invoked the intellectual legacy of founder Robert Menzies in their definitions of the 'sensible centre', the 'broad church' was looking to Foyle like flat-pack furniture assembled by incompetents (p. 145).

There have been qualified political bright spots for the Coalition this year: education reform in Gonski 2.0 (p. 98); the budget, though attacked from within as Labor-lite, finally got the government out from under the 2014 zombie measures (p. 124). The Snowy Mountain scheme was a significant 'announceable' (p. 88) that, along with large-scale battery storage, allowed Turnbull to slip back nostalgically into his old leather jacket persona (p. 91), but the Finkel report's recommendations on power, like every discussion on the topic in the last 10 years, became hostage to old arguments about climate change (p. 94).

Late in the year, cascading revelations about politicians' dual citizenship – and their rather perfunctory attitude to constititional requirements – entrenched in the public mind the chaos and dysfunction of our political class (p. 178). Though a problem not of the government's making, their response inspired little confidence. The spectacle of Julie Bishop provoking an international incident with New Zealand spoke of desperation (p. 182).

The other cardinal and totemic issue in the battle for the Liberal soul is same-sex marriage. The debate was reignited by the loose-lipped Christopher Pyne (p. 170) hinting at a strategy to achieve it, and gloating about the success of factional moderates – laying bare the fractures in the Coalition for all to see. The result

...FORGOTTEN PERSON...

PRYOR

Geoff Pryor, *The Saturday Paper*

Lindsay Foyle, *New Matilda*

will be decided, not simply by parliament or by Abbott's parting gift of a plebiscite — which would have had some electoral legitimacy — but in a non-binding postal survey (p. 176). The folly of all this is that the Coalition is tearing itself apart over an issue that most of the population either support or are indifferent to.

If same-sex marriage is a proxy for the liberal/conservative factional war, it is an issue, like climate policy, that makes Turnbull — the man who once impressed us by his willingness to stand and fall on principle — look weak, indecisive, hollow, and anyone's man but his own.

Pope depicts a shrunken leader incarcerated in the prison of his enemies' mind suffering a kind of political Stockholm syndrome (p. 39). Dyson captures the Turnbull predicament brilliantly with his prison mugshots of the conservative defector Cory Bernardi, the 'Conviction Conservative', alongside Turnbull, 'No Convictions Recorded' (p. 29). Of course, all politics requires compromise, but the prospect of a leader presiding over a range of policies we know he instinctively opposes must surely invite electoral retribution. If he survives that long.

As the government engages in a desperate search for the lost plot (p. 186), the Opposition is obeying a fundamental political rule — when your opponent is hell bent on self-destruction, sit back, keep quiet, and enjoy the mayhem (p. 184).

Did the man say 30 newspolls?

*

THIS YEAR we lost Bill Leak, one of out greatest cartoonists. I first met Bill while putting together the first edition of this book in 2003, and he has been a vital element in every collection since.

A hero, at various times, of both left and libertarian right, Bill remained an uncompromising controversialist to the end. Despite the extravagant and unbridled commentary immediately following his death, the longer-term assessment of Leak's rich artistic career — his incendiary cartoons and wonderfully insightful portraits — will be more measured and far kinder.

Like so many who knew him, I loved Bill's extraordinary warmth, his wicked brilliance, his openness, and his generosity. He was a man of enormous spirit. He will be greatly missed.

Vale Bill Leak.

Russ Radcliffe

Bill Leak, *The Australian*

David Rowe, *Australian Financial Review*

'Trump is the King Kong of shallowness: the only deep things about him are his roots in the American psyche. He brings forth not just the pout, the hair and the ties, but the greed, indulgence and psychotic menace of the *indigenous American berserk* … The mistake of his opponents – including the satirists – has been to focus on his otherness: in truth he's dredged straight from the brute material of American culture.'

– Don Watson

Geoff Pryor, *The Saturday Paper*

'The center core of what we believe, that we're a nation with an economy. Not an economy just in some global marketplace with open borders, but we are a nation with a culture and a reason for being.'
— Steve Bannon

'Just nothing better than calling out liberal jerk offs on Twitter. We won, you lost. You're done!'
— Roger Stone

'As democracy is perfected, the office of president represents, more and more closely, the inner soul of the people. On some great and glorious day the plain folks of the land will reach their heart's desire at last and the White House will be adorned by a downright moron.'
— H.L. Mencken

Andrew Dyson, *The Age*

Matt Golding, *The Sunday Age*

Judy Horacek, *The Age*

'I found much that was alarming about being a citizen during the tenures of Richard Nixon and George W. Bush. But, whatever I may have seen as their limitations of character or intellect, neither was anything like as humanly impoverished as Trump is: ignorant of government, of history, of science, of philosophy, of art, incapable of expressing or recognizing subtlety or nuance, destitute of all decency, and wielding a vocabulary of seventy-seven words that is better called Jerkish than English.'

— Philip Roth

Jon Kudelka, *The Mercury*

Andrew Dyson, *The Age*

David Rowe, *Australian Financial Review*

'I get up this morning, I turn on one of the networks, and they show an empty field. I say, wait a minute, I made a speech. I looked out, the field was — it looked like a million, million and a half people. They showed a field where there were practically nobody standing there. And they said, Donald Trump did not draw well. I said, it was almost raining, the rain should have scared them away, but God looked down and he said, we're not going to let it rain on your speech.'

— Donald Trump

'I play to people's fantasies ... People want to believe that something is the biggest and the greatest and the most spectacular. I call it truthful hyperbole. It's an innocent form of exaggeration — and it's a very effective form of promotion.'

— Trump, *The Art of the Deal*

"GOVERNMENT OF THE PENISES, BY THE PENISES, FOR THE PENISES."

Glen Le Lievre, *Crikey*

Matt Golding, *The Sunday Age*

David Rowe, *Australian Financial Review*

'We, assembled here today, are issuing a new decree to be heard in every city, in every foreign capital, and in every hall of power. From this day forward, a new vision will govern our land. From this moment on, it's going to be America First. Every decision on trade, on taxes, on immigration, on foreign affairs, will be made to benefit American workers and American families.'

— Donald Trump

'The world is in trouble, but we're gonna straighten it out, OK? That's what I do — I fix things. We're gonna straighten it out. Believe me.'

— Donald Trump

'This is thousands of times bigger, the United States, than the biggest company in the world.'

— Donald Trump

Matt Golding, *The Sunday Age*

Peter MacMullin, *Sunday Mail*

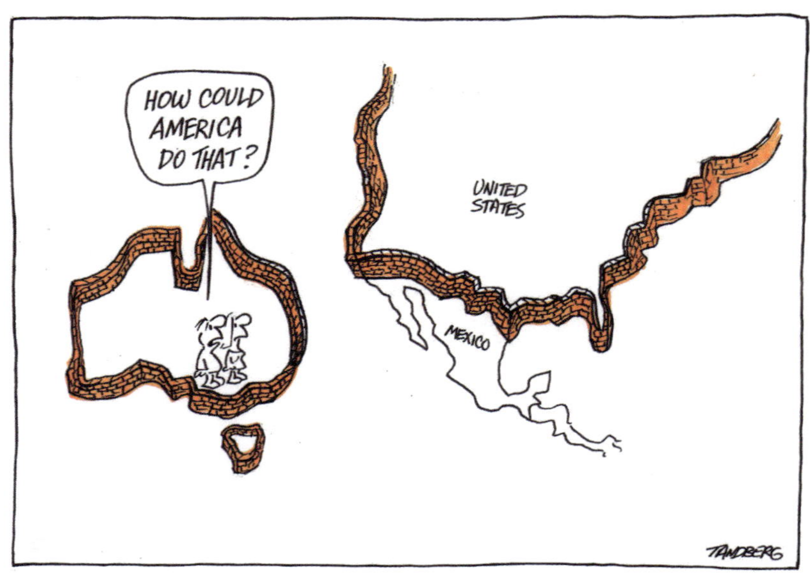

Ron Tandberg, *The Age*

Mark Knight, *Herald Sun*

Eric Löbbecke, *The Australian*

'Look, I spoke to Putin, Merkel, Abe of Japan, to France today, and this was my most unpleasant call because I will be honest with you. I hate taking these people. I guarantee you they are bad. That is why they are in prison right now.'

— Donald Trump

'We are going to have borders nice and strong. We are going to build a wall. You know that. Going to build the wall ... Mexico is going to pay for the wall. Right? It's going to happen. Going to happen. They know it. I know it. We all know it.'

— Donald Trump

'Donald J. Trump is calling for a complete and total shutdown of Muslims entering the United States until our country's representatives can figure out what the hell is going on.'

— Donald Trump

Peter Nicholson, *Australian Financial Review*

'We have a tremendous amount of respect for the people of Australia, for Prime Minister Trunbull.'
— Sean Spicer

'This is a better society than the United States ... the idea we should get around like Uriah Heep like we're some sort of subordinate outfit that has to get a signal from abroad before we think, is of course a complete denial of everything we've created here.'
— Paul Keating

'If you're going to pick on somebody who freeloads, you wouldn't pick on Australia. He is having that pointed out to him ... As this administration goes on, it's going to have to learn that it operates in an alliance environment, even if it wants to make America first.'
— Kim Beazley

Dean Alston, *The West Australian*

Mark Knight, *Herald Sun*

David Rowe, *Australian Financial Review*

Don Corleone: Someday, and that day may never come, I'll call upon you to do a service for me. But until that day, accept this justice as a gift on my daughter's wedding day.
Bonasera: Grazie, Godfather.
Don Corleone: Prego ...

Malcolm Turnbull: Thank you for your commitment. It is very important to us.
Donald Trump: It is important to you and it is embarrassing to me. It is an embarrassment to me, but at least I got you off the hook. So you put me back on the hook.
Malcolm Turnbull: You can count on me. I will be there again and again.
Donald Trump: I hope so. Okay, thank you Malcolm.

Cathy Wilcox, *The Sun-Herald*

Peter MacMullin, *Sunday Mail*

Alan Moir, *The Sydney Morning Herald*

Glen Le Lievre, *The Sun-Herald*

..DESPERATE FORMULA TO GET US OUT OF A POLITICAL HOLE...IN OUR TIME..

Geoff Pryor, *The Saturday Paper*

'Why is this so important? I do not understand. This is going to kill me. I am the world's greatest person that does not want to let people into the country. And now I am agreeing to take 2,000 people and I agree I can vet them ... It makes me look so bad and I have only been here a week.'

— Donald Trump

'I do believe that you will never find a better friend to the United States than Australia. I say this to you sincerely that it is in the mutual interest of the United States to say, "Yes, we can conform with that deal – we are not obliged to take anybody we do not want, we will go through extreme vetting" and that way you are seen to show the respect that a trusted ally wants and deserves.'

— Malcolm Turnbull

Fiona Katauskas, *New Matilda*

Matt Golding, *The Sunday Age*

Bill Leak, *The Australian*

Eric Löbbecke, *The Australian*

'You can say and think what you want, but because I am a free citizen of a free country and a member of a party which doesn't practise Stalinism, which believes in free speech, well, I'll say my piece ... No one should be bullied.'

— Tony Abbott

Cathy Wilcox, *The Sun-Herald*

Ron Tandberg, *The Age*

David Pope, *The Canberra Times*

'We are told time and time again that we must be tolerant … Well, I've had it up to here with my tolerance.'
— Pauline Hanson

'There is something permeating our culture right now that has led to a loss of identity for men in particular … For centuries we have known, because of biological reasons, what our place in the world was. Men were the hunters, women the gatherers. Men were the protectors, women the nurturers.'
— George Christensen

'What the government needs to do is not to overreact to Hanson but to get on with the job of being a strong and sensible centre-right government. This is exactly what John Howard did after the 1998 election when One Nation got a very strong vote.'
— Tony Abbott

Matt Golding, *The Sunday Age*

Peter Broelman, *www.broelman.com.au*

Alan Moir, *The Sydney Morning Herald*

Sean Leahy, *The Courier Mail*

Andrew Dyson, *The Age*

'The level of public disenchantment with the major parties, lack of confidence in our political process, and concern about the direction of our nation is very strong. This is a direct product of the political class being out of touch with the hopes and aspirations of the Australian people.'

— Senator Cory Bernardi

'While Cory and I have sometimes disagreed, I'm disappointed that more effort has not been made to keep our party united.'

— Tony Abbott, MP

'It really is time for a better way — for a conservative way.'

— Senator Cory Bernardi

'Breaking faith with the electorate, breaking faith with the people who voted for you, breaking faith with the people who have supported you through thick and thin for years, is not a conservative thing to do.'

— George Brandis, Attorney-General

Dean Alston, *The West Australian*

'The WA election shows there isn't a vast bulk of reactionary voters waiting to be embraced as part of the mainstream. The Liberal-National Coalition is at its best when it starts from its centre-right mainstream base and reaches into the mainstream middle – not when it legitimises the fringes. When we do a preference deal with One Nation we legitimise them and get distracted as the folly of many of their policies are exposed.'

— Tim Wilson, MP

'Doing the deal with the Libs has done damage to us, in all honesty. It was a mistake ... We are really going to have to have a good look at this because all I heard all day leading up to this election was, 'Why are you sending your preferences to the Liberal Party?'

— Senator Pauline Hanson

Jon Kudelka, *www.kudelka.com.au*

Mark Knight, *Herald Sun*

Dean Alston, *The West Australian*

'I've got no problems with Vladimir ... Vladimir Putin and Donald Trump are strong leaders. You may not agree with what they do, but they are prepared to make a decision and they have the country's best interests at heart. That's what people want from leaders here in this nation.'

— Pauline Hanson

'The One Nation of today is a very different beast to what it was 20 years ago. They're a lot more sophisticated.'

— Arthur Sinodinos

'What I don't like about it is the blackmailing that's happening with the government. Don't do that to people. That's a dictatorship. I think people have a right to investigate themselves.'

— Pauline Hanson on vaccination

'This bat poo crazy stuff does not help anybody.'

— Barnaby Joyce

Paul Zanetti, *www.zanetti.net.au*

Jon Kudelka, *The Australian*

Fiona Katauskas, *New Matilda*

Peter MacMullin, *Sunday Mail*

'Rod, excuse me, I'm party leader. I expect you to come to my office, right.'
— Pauline Hanson

'I don't need her consent on every email that I send out of this office, I'm the boss of this office.'
— Rod Culleton

'He is not a team player at all. We can't work with him; you can't reason with him and honestly I think the whole lot has gone to his head.'
— Pauline Hanson

'I have played a lot of football in my life and I have never, ever seen Pauline Hanson at one of my football matches.'
— Rod Culleton

First Dog on the Moon, *The Guardian*

Glen Le Lievre, *Crikey*

'There is an opportunity for us to make some money on this if we play this smart.'
— James Ashby

'Between the printing contracts, the plane, and this apparent attempt to rip off taxpayers what we're seeing is that Pauline Hanson and James Ashby are in this to benefit themselves.'
— Senator Murray Watt

'I want to see Ashby go down in flames because I think he'll bring her down in flames, I really do.'
— Diane Happ, former One Nation candidate

'They're just another grubby, dirty, bloody political party that are out to serve their own ends, their own interests.'
— Dane Sorensen, former One Nation candidate

Jon Kudelka, *The Australian*

Matt Golding, *The Sunday Age*

David Pope, *The Canberra Times*

'We should make no apology for asking those who seek to join our Australian family to join us as Australian patriots – committed to the values that define us, committed to the values that unite us. … There is no more important title in our democracy than "Australian citizen"'.

– Malcolm Turnbull

'For too long, the good people of our country have been too tolerant of people who do not share some of the fundamental values that have made us who we are … a majority that stays silent does not stay a majority.'

– Tony Abbott

'If English grammar is the test, there might be a few members of parliament who might struggle.'

– Penny Wong

'They hate Western society. They want to change us. Do you want to be changed?'

– Pauline Hanson

First Dog on the Moon, *The Guardian*

Reg Lynch, *The Sun-Herald*

'You basically leave people alone; if they're not annoying you, don't annoy them. We are robust. If someone wants to stride around in a pair of shorts and a t-shirt you let them. We roll with the punches. We believe that if one person wants to have a beer, they can. If another person decides they don't want to, that's completely and utterly their choice.'

— Barnaby Joyce

'If you hate your country so much [you] mock its values on social media, you should think long and hard about your own citizenship.'

— George Christensen, MP

'Populism is the enemy of pluralism. It feeds into ideas of the "real people" or the "non-people".'

— Timothy Garton Ash, philosopher

David Pope, *The Canberra Times*

Matt Golding, *The Sunday Age*

Alan Moir, *The Sydney Morning Herald*

'The advice I have is that out of the last 33 people who have been charged with terrorist-related offences in this country, 22 of those people are from second- and third-generation Lebanese–Muslim background.'

— Peter Dutton

'If there is a particular problem that people can point to within a certain community ... then clearly mistakes have been made in the past ... The reality is that Malcolm Fraser did make mistakes in bringing some people in in the 1970s and we're seeing that today. We need to be honest in having that discussion.'

— Peter Dutton

'Our hardworking migrant communities shouldn't have to tolerate this kind of ignorant stupidity, and he needs to immediately apologise.'

— Bill Shorten

Pat Campbell, *The Canberra Times*

'Lest. We. Forget. (Manus, Nauru, Syria, Palestine ...)'
— Yassmin Abdel-Magied, Anzac Day Facebook post)

'Yassmin Abdel Magied's attacks on our democracy ... and effectively backing Arab dictatorships where forced marriages, female genital mutilation, and sexuality-based executions are legal are reprehensible. If Ms Abdel-Magied thinks our system of government is so bad, perhaps she should stop being a drain on the taxpayer and move to one of these Arab dictatorships that are so welcoming of women.'
— Eric Abetz

'Given that I am now the most publicly hated Muslim in Australia, people have been asking me how I am. What do I say? That life has been great ... That I've been overwhelmed with messages of support? Or do I tell them that it's been thoroughly rubbish? That it is humiliating to have almost 90,000 twisted words written about me in the three months since Anzac Day, words that are largely laced with hate.'
— Yassmin Abdel-Magied

Fiona Katauskas, *New Matilda*

First Dog on the Moon, *The Guardian*

Reg Lynch, *The Sun-Herald*

'Islam is a disease; we need to vaccinate ourselves against that.'
— Senator Pauline Hanson

'One Nation wants to shut down migration to Australia based on racial and religious prejudice. It wants to turn back history, to restore Australia to some imagined earlier state as a uniform, homogenous, static society. This is not just a narrow-minded and impoverished vision for the future. It is also based on a myth about Australia's past.'
— Penny Wong

'Hopes can be disappointed. Nostalgia is irrefutable.'
— Mark Lilla

Bill Leak, *The Australian*

'So now there's a mob that won't only punish you if your cartoon offends them, they'll punish you if it's offended someone else. They're also driven by the same authoritarian impulse to silence … anyone who transgresses against the unwritten laws of political correctness.'

— Bill Leak

'I think political correctness has become a problem … we've become far too apologetic about our Western identity and … defence of cultural traditionalism or national identity is in many ways frowned upon.'

— John Howard

'Whether it's official persecution of Queensland students for a bit of justified sarcasm, state governments promoting gender fluidity programs in schools, or a federal government-approved activist being disrespectful of Anzac Day, there's this pervasive ambivalence verging on hostility to our country and its values from people who should know better.'

— Tony Abbott

Bill Leak, *The Australian*

Bill Leak, *The Australian*

Matt Golding, *The Sunday Age*

Alan Moir, *The Sydney Morning Herald*

Geoff Pryor, *The Saturday Paper*

'I think there was concern about why the boy was being led, or for what purpose he was being led, away back into the regional processing centre ... I think it's fair to say that the mood had elevated quite quickly. I think some of the local residents were quite angry about this particular incident and another alleged sexual assault. Again, I don't have the full details and those matters are under investigation.'

— Peter Dutton

'To those who dragged and forced us to airplane from Christmas Island/Darwin and dropped us to Manus Island: We people have been detained on Manus Island for about four years against our will, are requesting to be moved to some safe place ... Everyone is terrified due to current attack by PNG defence forces by machine guns, our lives is in danger.'

— asylum-seekers' letter, Manus Island

First Dog on the Moon, *The Guardian*

Geoff Pryor, *The Saturday Paper*

'Last November, UNHCR exceptionally agreed to help with the relocation of refugees to the United States following a bilateral agreement between Australia and the US ... We agreed to do so on the clear understanding that vulnerable refugees with close family ties in Australia would ultimately be allowed to settle there ... [But] UNHCR has recently been informed by Australia that it refuses to accept even these refugees. This means, for example, that some with serious medical conditions, or who have undergone traumatic experiences, including sexual violence, cannot receive the support of their close family members residing in Australia.'

— Filippo Grandi, UNHCR

'The position of the Coalition government has been clear and consistent: those transferred to regional processing centres will never settle in Australia.'

— Spokesperson for Peter Dutton

Alan Moir, *The Sydney Morning Herald*

'Our foreign policy has been a disaster. We've neglected and abandoned our allies. We've emboldened our enemies. The message I have — it's a very simple one. It's a bumper sticker, Sean: The era of the Pajama Boy is over January 20th, and the alpha males are back.'

— Sebastian Gorka, White House national security aide

'For those who don't have our back, we're taking names.'

— Nikki Haley, US ambassador to the UN

'Donald Trump is the most ill-informed, under-prepared, ethically challenged, and psychologically ill-equipped president in US history. He has led an administration acting so far on the basis of postures rather than policies. While the commentariat is beginning to find some comforting early signs that the adults are regaining charge of foreign policy, anyone betting on this administration delivering consistent, coherent, constructive, and decent outcomes over the next four years is making a very big gamble indeed.'

— Gareth Evans

Andrew Weldon, *Big Issue*

John Farmer, *Sunday Tasmanian*

'The third, broadly, line of work is deconstruction of the administrative state. ... If you look at these cabinet appointees, they were selected for a reason and that is the deconstruction. The way the progressive left runs is, if they can't get it passed, they're just going to put in some sort of regulation in an agency. That's all going to be deconstructed.'

— Steve Bannon

'Of course, the Deep State exists. There's a permanent state of massive bureaucracies that do whatever they want and set up deliberate leaks to attack the president. ... This is what the Deep State does: They create a lie, spread a lie, fail to check the lie and then deny that they were behind the lie.'

— Newt Gingrich

'It's time for the Trump administration to begin to purge these saboteurs before it's too late.'

— Sean Hannity, Fox News

Glen Le Lievre, *Crikey*

Cathy Wilcox, *The Sun-Herald*

'When I see a story about "Donald Trump didn't fill hundreds and hundreds of jobs," it's because, in many cases, we don't want to fill those jobs. A lot of those jobs, I don't want to appoint, because they're unnecessary to have. You know, we have so many people in government, even me. I look at some of the jobs and it's people over people over people. I say, "What do all these people do?" You don't need all those jobs.'

— Donald Trump

'I don't think this administration thinks the State Department needs to exist. They think Jared [Kushner] can do everything. It's reminiscent of the developing countries where I've served. The family rules everything, and the Ministry of Foreign Affairs knows nothing.'

— State Department staffer

'It's time to admit that Washington is Baghdad on the Potomac. The branches of government are at war with one another, and no one knows where the Green Zone is.'

— *Newsweek*

Eric Löbbecke, *The Australian*

Bill O'Reilly: Putin's a killer.
Donald Trump: There are a lot of killers. You think our country is so innocent?

'They either don't understand that they are harming their country – which makes them just dumb – or they understand, which makes them dangerous and dirty.'
— Vladimir Putin

Sean Leahy, *The Courier Mail*

Ron Tandberg, *The Age*

Matt Golding, *The Sunday Age*

'While I greatly appreciate you informing me, on three separate occasions, that I am not under investigation, I nevertheless must concur with the Department of Justice that you are not able to effectively lead the Bureau.'

— Donald Trump

'James Comey better hope that there are no 'tapes' of our conversations before he starts leaking to the press!'

— Donald Trump

'It's very Nixonian, in its own way, but that's typical of the man. They're obviously trying the get the Bureau back under the Department of Justice's control. But I don't think it'll affect the Russia investigation. You've got too many career people, and the counter-intelligence division — the cream of the crop — that will not take lightly to being messed with.'

— John Dean, Richard Nixon's White House counsel

Cathy Wilcox, *The Sun-Herald*

Jos Valdman, *The Advertiser*

Matt Golding, *The Sunday Age*

'Only the Fake News Media and Trump enemies want me to stop using Social Media (110 million people). Only way for me to get the truth out!'
— Donald Trump

'They get started by suppressing free press ... when you look at history, the first thing that dictators do is shut down the press. And I'm not saying that President Trump is trying to be a dictator. I'm just saying we need to learn the lessons of history.'
— John McCain

'The American fascist would prefer not to use violence. His method is to poison the channels of public information.'
— Henry A. Wallace, 1944

Christopher Downes, *The Mercury*

Pat Campbell, *The Canberra Times*

Ron Tandberg, *The Age*

'We're not going into Syria. But when I see people using horrible, horrible chemical weapons ... and see these beautiful kids that are dead in their father's arms, or you see kids gasping for life ... when you see that, I immediately called General Mattis.'

— Donald Trump

'We didn't use chemical weapons in World War II. You know, you had a — someone as despicable as Hitler who didn't even sink to using chemical weapons.'

— Sean Spicer

'As a whole, the administration's stance with regards to Syria remains a mystery. Inconsistency is what comes to mind first of all.'

— Sergei Ryabkov, Russian deputy foreign minister

Cathy Wilcox, *The Sun-Herald*

Christopher Downes, *The Mercury*

David Rowe, *Australian Financial Review*

'I was sitting at the table. We had finished dinner. We're now having dessert. And we had the most beautiful piece of chocolate cake that you've ever seen and President Xi was enjoying it. And I was given the message from the generals that the ships are locked and loaded, what do you do? And we made a determination to do it, so the missiles were on the way. And I said, Mr. President, let me explain something to you. This was during dessert. We've just fired 59 missiles, all of which hit, by the way, unbelievable, from, you know, hundreds of miles away, all of which hit, amazing.'

— Donald Trump

'I am very disappointed in China. Our foolish past leaders have allowed them to make hundreds of billions of dollars a year in trade, yet they do nothing for us with North Korea, just talk. We will no longer allow this to continue. China could easily solve this problem!'

— Donald Trump

Matt Golding, *The Sunday Age*

Dean Alston, *The West Australian*

David Pope, *The Canberra Times*

'Trump is quite a personality, and he likes to tweet. But emotional venting cannot become a guiding policy for solving the nuclear issue on the peninsula.'
— *Xinhua News Agency*

'North Korea is ready to react to any mode of war desired by the US.'
— North Korean spokesman

'North Korea is looking for trouble. If China decides to help, that would be great. If not, we will solve the problem without them!'
— Donald Trump

'In general, primitiveness and loutishness are very characteristic of the current rhetoric coming out of Washington. We'll hope that this doesn't become the substance of American policy.'
— Sergei Ryabkov, Russian deputy foreign minister

Dean Alston, *The West Australian*

Andrew Weldon, *Big Issue*

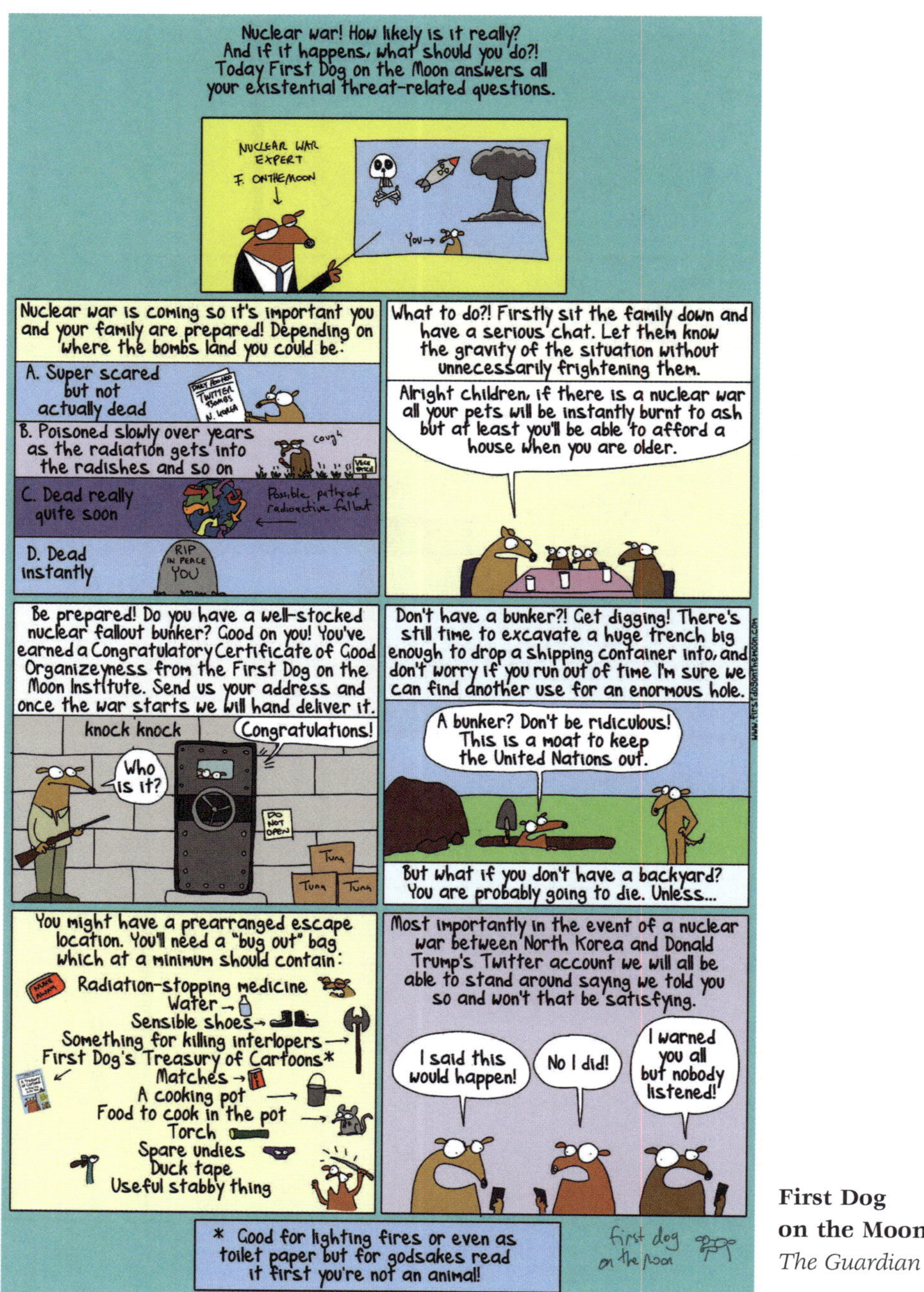

First Dog on the Moon, *The Guardian*

Pat Campbell, *The Canberra Times*

'We'll handle North Korea. We'll be able to handle North Korea. It will be handled. We handle everything.'
— Donald Trump

'The patience of the United States and our allies in this region has run out and we want to see change. We want to see North Korea abandon its reckless path of the development of nuclear weapons, and also its continual use and testing of ballistic missiles is unacceptable. But as the president has made very clear, either China will deal with this problem or the United States and our allies will.'
— Mike Pence

'Japan, South Korea, China would all be in the crosshairs of a war if we started one with North Korea. But if [North Korea gets] a missile they can hit California, maybe other parts of America … If there's going to be a war to stop [Kim Jong-un], it will be over there. If thousands die, they're going to die over there. They're not going to die here.'
— Lindsey Graham

David Rowe, *Australian Financial Review*

'When I sit around the negotiating table in the months ahead, I will represent every person in the United Kingdom — young and old, rich and poor, city, town, country, and all the villages and hamlets in between. It is my fierce determination to get the right deal for every single person in this country. For, as we face the opportunities ahead of us on this momentous journey, our shared values, interests, and ambitions can — and must — bring us together.'

— Theresa May

'We have realized in the past few months that Europe is more than just bureaucracy and economic regulation, that Europe and living together in the European Union have something to do with war and peace, that the decades of peace after World War II would have been completely unthinkable without the European Union. ... And that's why it is worth fighting for this Europe.'

— Angela Merkel

Paul Zanetti, *www.zanetti.net.au*

Jos Valdman, *The Advertiser*

Geoff Pryor, *The Saturday Paper*

'There are two kinds of European nations. There are small nations and there are countries that have not yet realised they are small nations.'

— Kristian Jensen, Danish finance minister

'There is no need to pretend that this is a happy day, neither in Brussels nor in London. After all, most Europeans, including almost half the British voters, wish that we would stay together, not drift apart.'

— Donald Tusk, president of the European council

'This is the richest borough in our country treating its citizens in this way and we should call it what it is. It is corporate manslaughter. And there should be arrests made; frankly, it is an outrage.'

— David Lammy, MP on Grenfell Tower fire

Cathy Wilcox, *The Sun-Herald*

David Pope, *The Canberra Times*

Cathy Wilcox, *The Sun-Herald*

Christopher Downes, *The Mercury*

Alan Moir, *The Sydney Morning Herald*

'Londoners will see an increased police presence today and over the course of the next few days. No reason to be alarmed.'

— Sadiq Khan, London mayor

'At least 7 dead and 48 wounded in terror attack and Mayor of London says there is "no reason to be alarmed!"'

— Donald Trump

'It's called leadership, Donald. The terrorists were dead 8 minutes after police got the call. If we need an alarmist blowhard, we'll call.'

— J. K. Rowling

'People are feeling sorry for people over there and I've seen the hashtag #prayforlondon ... I have my own hashtag and you won't need to be praying for this place or that place, because it's #pray4amuslimban.'

— Pauline Hanson

Dean Alston, *The West Australian*

John Farmer, *The Mercury*

Alan Moir, *The Sydney Morning Herald*

Jon Kudelka, *The Mercury*

'If I was going to change the date, it would be June the 3rd, which is the day when terra nullius was struck down — that's a day worth celebrating. Because all the lies we've suffered from began with terra nullius — that this was nobody's land — which was a doozy.'

— June Mills, Larrakia elder

'I'm just sick of these people who every time they want to make us feel guilty about it. They don't like Christmas, they don't like Australia Day, they're just miserable ... and I wish they'd crawl under a rock and hide ... Don't start your weeping and gnashing your teeth around me about the terrible evil that we've done.'

— Barnaby Joyce

'I believe the road to reconciliation is a process, it's a journey. There are many bigger and more profound issues, including constitutional recognition, to deal with than the date of Australia Day.'

— Malcolm Turnbull

Fiona Katauskas, *Eureka Street*

Geoff Pryor, *The Saturday Paper*

David Rowe, *Australian Financial Review*

'We have nothing more to give you. We give you a ceremony, and our leaders didn't get it, they can just stand here and give empty platitudes.'
— Pat Anderson

'Changing the Australian constitution is not easy ... History would indicate that to succeed, not only must there be overwhelming support, but minimal — or at least tepid — opposition.'
— Malcolm Turnbull

'The Prime Minister had an opportunity today to say, "I stand with our First Nation people, I've heard them and we are going to work towards a treaty and towards a strong Aboriginal voice", and instead he appears to have backed away from any significant change.'
— Richard Di Natale

Cathy Wilcox, *The Sun-Herald*

Peter Broelman, *www.broelman.com.au*

Mark Knight, *Herald Sun*

'We don't make sure we have enough scotch fillet in the supermarket by telling farmers they can't sell their beef or cattle to overseas markets, right? We let them sell to a wide range of markets, which gives them confidence to invest, which gives them a good return when they can get a good price – and we have plenty of steak.'

— Matt Canavan

'Along comes a carbon tax. It wasn't a carbon tax, as you know. It was many other things in nomenclature terms but we made it a carbon tax. We made it a fight about the hip pocket and not about the environment. That was brutal retail politics and it took Abbott about six months to cut through and when he cut through, Gillard was gone.'

— Peta Credlin

'I have a position that is very clear, that we will not be adopting an emissions intensity scheme.'

— Josh Frydenberg

Peter Nicholson, *Australian Financial Review*

Matt Golding, *The Sunday Age*

First Dog on the Moon, *The Guardian*

David Pope, *The Canberra Times*

Bill Leak, *The Australian*

Mark Knight, *Herald Sun*

'The Turnbull Government will start work on an electricity game-changer: the plan for the Snowy Mountains Scheme 2.0 ... For too long, policymakers have put ideology and politics ahead of engineering and economics. Successive governments at all levels have failed to put in place the necessary storage to ensure reliable power supply to homes and businesses ... By supercharging the Snowy Hydro precinct, we can ensure affordable and reliable electricity for Australian households and businesses.'

— Malcolm Turnbull

'There were discussions with the prime minister's office, I think on the 3rd or the 5th of March. And the announcement was on the 16th of March.'

— Paul Broad, Snowy Hydro CEO

'I am not into political slogans. I am into engineering and economics.'

— Malcolm Turnbull

David Pope, *The Canberra Times*

Alan Moir, *The Sydney Morning Herald*

David Pope, *The Canberra Times*

Peter MacMullin, *Sunday Mail*

"I CAN'T INVITE YOU IN, BUT THANKS FOR FINDING MY JACKET."

Glen Le Lievre, *Crikey*

'The next incarnation of our national energy policy should be technology agnostic — it's security and cost that matter most, not how you deliver it.'

— Malcolm Turnbull

'South Australia joins the likes of California as a world leader in demonstrating how renewable energy and storage technologies can power our economy cheaply and cleanly.'

— Tim Flannery

'What Australians need is wise leadership, not glib leadership. Glibness is not going to keep the lights on.'

— Malcolm Turnbull

David Rowe, *Australian Financial Review*

'Australian coal can be used everywhere except Australia. It doesn't make much sense.'
— Tony Abbott

'Storage has a big role to play, that's true, but we will need more synchronous baseload power, and as the world's largest coal exporter we have a vested interest in showing that we can provide both lower emissions and reliable base-load power with state-of-the-art clean-coal-fired technology.'
— Malcolm Turnbull

'If we decide that we don't want to use Adani — the coal from the Galilee coalfields — to help poor people in India be able to turn on their lights like we do, they're still going to get coal. They're just going to get coal that's 60 per cent less efficient, from India.'
— Barnaby Joyce

David Pope, *The Canberra Times*

Fiona Katauskas, *Eureka Street*

Mark Knight, *Herald Sun*

'There are two criteria ...when we judge the Finkel report. First, do its proposals take the pressure off power prices, because prices should be going down, not up? And second, does it allow coal to continue? ... Now, we all know that there is no such thing as a magic pudding, and if you are rewarding one type of energy, inevitably that money's got to come from somewhere ... it's effectively a tax on coal, and that's the last thing we want.'

— Tony Abbott

'When you start employing Tony Abbott's climate targets, what you end up with is a finishing line where you're going to see coal and gas burning until 2070 ... What we're doing is, we're saying we've got a climate crisis ... There's no point in having certainty if we lose the Great Barrier Reef, if we end up in a warming world where we see more extreme weather, heatwaves, cyclones, bushfires.'

— Senator Richard Di Natale

Cathy Wilcox, *The Sun-Herald*

Sean Leahy, *The Courier Mail*

Peter Broelman, *www.broelman.com.au*

'Now, the empirical evidence, which is what is the only thing that decides science, shows that we can't even affect the level of carbon dioxide in the atmosphere and that carbon dioxide in the atmosphere is a result of temperature change, not a cause of that.'

— Senator Malcolm Roberts

'All the scientists I know have a healthy degree of scepticism, but healthy is an important word there. You have to have an open mind, but not so open your brain leaks out.'

— Alan Finkel

'I'm aware of who Malcolm Roberts is, and the only surprise is that he is in fact a senator.'

— Gavin Schmidt, NASA GISS director

'We really are in a very Kafka-esque world ... I need a biscuit.'

— Arthur Sinodinos

Judy Horacek, *The Age*

Judy Horacek, *The Age*

Andrew Weldon, *Big Issue*

Mark Knight, *Herald Sun*

'The Turnbull government will deliver the real "Gonski" needs-based funding model that Labor didn't. We will end Labor's 27 special deals with states and territories, unions, and non-government school leaders. Labor traded away the principles of the "Gonski" report for political expediency.'

— Malcolm Turnbull

'This is a very big change of policy ... It certainly hasn't gone to the party room, and I imagine this will be pretty vigorously debated in the party room next week.'

— Tony Abbott

'The big picture here is that in the 2014 budget, Tony Abbott promised a $30 billion cut to our schools, and in the 2017 budget, Malcolm Turnbull wants a big pat on the back for changing that cut to a $22 billion cut. A week out from the federal budget, this is taking out the trash.'

— Tanya Plibersek

Pat Campbell, *The Canberra Times*

Sean Leahy, *The Courier Mail*

Glen Le Lievre, *The Sydney Morning Herald*

'I call on the Labor Party to stop the scare campaign and support fair school funding into the future. Stop worrying principals, teachers, parents, or others with needless lies.'
— Simon Birmingham, education minister

'There has been no consultation with schools or state governments on this.'
— Meredith Peace, Australian Education Union

'Knowing a little bit about politics, I suspect that the government will decide that it's on a loser if it does anything that looks like it's disadvantaging Catholic schools.'
— Tony Abbott

'This is delivering on that great vision of David Gonski's.'
— Malcolm Turnbull

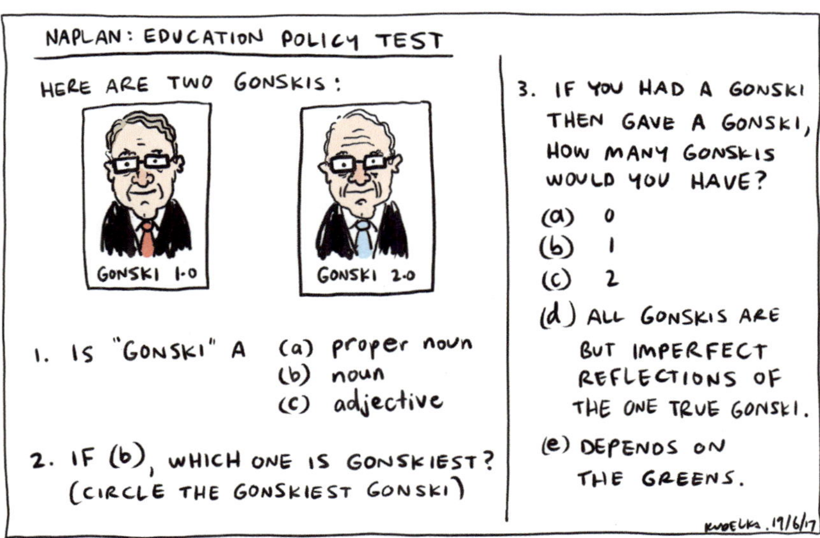

Jon Kudelka, *The Australian*

David Pope, *The Canberra Times*

Jon Kudelka, *The Australian*

'People are sick of the argy-bargy between the states and the federal government, they're sick of the hyper-partisan fights between the government and the opposition, we've got to get the politics out of this.'
— Sarah Hanson-Young

'This leaflet was in circulation when the leader and the portfolio holder ... were in discussions with the government [about] securing billions of dollars of additional funding for underfunded public schools. Clearly, this leaflet had the potential to damage those negotiations.'
— Senator Richard Di Natale et al

'We are disappointed in the party room's eagerness to cruelly and publicly undermine NSW's Greens senator for simply taking the position of her party, and a policy the Greens took to an election.'
— NSW Greens

'When it comes to political white-anting, Lee is the Greens' version of Tony Abbott.'
— Bob Brown

Mark Knight, *Herald Sun*

David Pope, *The Canberra Times*

David Rowe, *Australian Financial Review*

'We're not asking people to move to Kathmandu or Timbuktu.'
— Barnaby Joyce on APVMA relocation

'We've published some new talking points for you to use in social settings which will help you discuss our relocation to Armidale with friends and family ... the BBQ conversation:

"(I'm pretty sure I'll be relocating to Armidale) I'm listening to what our executive have to say about the transition, but for the moment I'm getting on with the job."'
— Stefanie Janiec, APVMA chief operating officer

'I don't think it's a disaster and I think it is going well. I think Barnaby Joyce has been very courageous in moving the APVMA out there. It's been a very bold move ... It wasn't pork barrelling at all.'
— Fiona Nash

Alan Moir, *The Sydney Morning Herald*

Jon Kudelka, *The Australian*

Sean Leahy, *The Courier Mail*

'It was an entirely incidental and unplanned activity, to what was an otherwise busy weekend schedule. The first time that I saw the apartment was 20 minutes before the auction commenced.'
— Sussan Ley

'Australians are entitled to expect that politicians spend taxpayers' money carefully, ensuring at all times that their work expenditure represents an efficient, effective, and ethical use of public resources. We should be, as politicians, backbenchers and ministers, we should be as careful and as accountable with taxpayers' money as we possibly can be.'
— Malcolm Turnbull

'I am not going to be someone who judges her. She should not be attacked like people behaving like a pack of dogs. I do know that there are socialists out there who want to attack free enterprise and anyone who sticks up for it. I know that socialists, like alcoholics, will blame anyone but themselves. Whereas alcoholics can damage their own family, socialists can destroy the whole country.'
— Bronwyn Bishop

Greg Smith, *The Sunday Times*

Greg Smith, *The Sunday Times*

Peter Broelman, *www.broelman.com.au*

'Why did I ask them to pay? To avoid paying a $1,670 bill myself. It was wrong and a big mistake.'
— Senator Sam Dastayari

'But Sam, how you could accept money in a public position for private accounts just defies any standard whatsoever. I'm just astounded that you did it.'
— Senator Eric Abetz

'People do need to work after they leave parliament.'
— Scott Ryan, special minister of state, on Andrew Robb's post-politics career

'The revelations that foreign governments are buying influence in Australia once again demonstrates just how critical it is that the government and Bill Shorten support our legislation for a federal ICAC, comprehensive donations reform, and a five-year ban on former ministers working as lobbyists.'
— Richard Di Natale

Cathy Wilcox, *The Sun-Herald*

ELECTION SCRUTINEERING

Peter Broelman, *www.broelman.com.au*

David Pope, *The Canberra Times*

'Centrelink is simply doing what has been done for years – cross checking Tax Office income information against what welfare recipients have self-reported to Centrelink. The only major change is that it is more automated so we can complete more checks ... At any point in the process, an individual can call a Centrelink officer for assistance.'

– Alan Tudge, human services minister

'Customers must be encouraged to self-manage as assistance is intended for vulnerable customers or those with extenuating circumstances.'

– Centrelink memo

'It is as if Centrelink has simply decided that their prized data-matching program is now too hard, too time consuming and too costly ... So let's outsource it to the customer – they will be so overwhelmed that they will give up.'

– Centrelink employee

Andrew Dyson, *The Age*

Jon Kudelka, *The Mercury*

First Dog on the Moon, *The Guardian*

Alan Moir, *The Sydney Morning Herald*

'The Minister for Human Services must step in today personally and direct Centrelink to stop this ham-fisted approach. If the system can't be quickly fixed then it must be at least deactivated until the problems are sorted out.'

— Andrew Wilkie

'Labor is demanding we cease a process that has successfully recovered over $300 million of incorrectly paid taxpayers money since July and, frankly, I don't think many taxpayers would support that call.'

— Alan Tudge

'The rest of the committee came away from this deeply distressed and concerned about how people have been affected by this. They knew they were sending out letters to people who didn't have debts — they didn't have a human checking them.'

— Rachel Siewart, Senate committee

'The system was so flawed that it was set up to fail.'

— Senate committee

Peter Nicholson, *Australian Financial Review*

'I have seen young people order smashed avocado with crumbled feta on five-grain toasted bread at $22 a pop and more ... how can young people afford to eat like this?'

— Bernard Salt

'Liberal economics ... dramatically increased wealth around the world ... But since 2008, [it] has gone nowhere ... We have a comatose world economy held together by debt and central bank money ... Liberal economics has run into a dead end and has had no answer to the contemporary malaise.'

— Paul Keating

'A big slowdown in immigration would allow housing and infrastructure to catch up with population. It would give harder-to-assimilate recent migrants more time to integrate with the wider Australian community before many more came in.'

— Tony Abbott

Andrew Dyson, *The Age*

Pat Campbell, *The Canberra Times*

Peter Nicholson, *Australian Financial Review*

'Australians understand taking out a mortgage to pay for their home is a wise investment for their future. But they also know that putting your everyday expenses on the credit card is not a good idea. It doesn't end well. That is basically the difference between good and bad debt. The same is true for government.'

— Scott Morrison

'One of the great somersaults with pike in Australian history I think, the Scott Morrison good-debt, bad-debt conversion ... [He] is setting up an excuse and an alibi for his failure when it comes to debt. He doesn't actually believe in infrastructure. If he did, there would be more infrastructure projects in the budget. He had a $10 billion rail fund in the budget, he wrote out a list of projects, and he did not fund one of them. Not one dollar.'

— Chris Bowen

Peter MacMullin, *Sunday Mail*

Glen Le Lievre, *The Sydney Morning Herald*

David Rowe, *Australian Financial Review*

'The adjustments to Sunday penalty rates will even the playing field for Australia's small businesses [and] help thousands of small businesses open their doors, serve customers, and create jobs on Sundays.'

— Michaelia Cash

'This is an appalling decision and comes at a time when wages are falling in real terms … It doesn't matter if the cuts are phased in over two or three years, the damage is the same.'

— Bill Shorten

'There is rampant lawlessness in the workplaces of Australia, and this is occurring in the form of chronic underpayments of workers, exploitation of visa workers, and workplace practices that put the safety and lives of people at risk.'

— Sally McManus, ACTU secretary

Cathy Wilcox, *The Sun-Herald*

John Farmer, *Sunday Tasmanian*

First Dog on the Moon, *The Guardian*

Matt Bissett-Johnson, *Melbourne Observer*

Matt Bissett-Johnson, *Melbourne Observer*

Cathy Wilcox, *The Sun-Herald*

'I believe in the rule of law when the law, is fair and the law is right ... But when it's unjust, I don't think there's a problem with breaking it.'

— Sally McManus, ACTU secretary

'Militant unions have used bullying and standover tactics to trash the rule of law on work sites, and now one of Australia's most senior union bosses says the law should only apply when you agree with it.'

— Malcolm Turnbull

'Every single Australian benefits from superannuation, Medicare, the weekend, and minimum wages — these were all won by our parents, grandparents, and great-grandparents taking non-violent so-called illegal industrial action.'

— Sally McManus, ACTU secretary

'The kind of anarchic Marxist clap trap we used to hear from anarchists at Adelaide University in the 1980s.'

— Christopher Pyne

Jon Kudelka, *The Mercury*

Sean Leahy, *The Courier Mail*

Alan Moir, *The Sydney Morning Herald*

'So to be clear, our plan is: to grow our economy to create more and better-paid jobs, to guarantee the essentials that Australians rely on, to reduce cost-of-living pressures, and to ensure that the government lives within its means. Once again Mr Speaker, I commend our plan, this budget, and this bill to the House.'

— Scott Morrison

'Just at this moment, let me tell you, we're at a bit of a low ebb … If you listen to some senior members of the government, because of the reality — the unfortunate reality — of the Senate, we have had to bring forward a budget which is second-best. A taxing and spending budget. Not because we believe in these things, but because the Senate made us do it. Well, a party that has to do what's second-best because the Senate made us do it is a party which needs some help.'

— Tony Abbott

'Practical governments deal with problems and solve them. This is not a budget for ideologues; this is a budget for a government that is doing its job.'

— Scott Morrison

Andrew Dyson, *The Age*

Andrew Dyson, *The Age*

David Rowe, *Australian Financial Review*

'I don't think we should be under any illusions here – this is a money grab from a sector of the economy that the government thinks is an easy target, and there should be no illusions about what this is.'

— Anna Bligh, Australian Bankers' Association

'As every business owner or employee knows, every extra cost needs to be borne by customers or shareholders, or a combination of both.'

— Ian Narev, Commonwealth Bank of Australia

'No one should want to increase taxes, even on banks. I can certainly understand the banks fighting back.'

— Tony Abbott

Jon Kudelka, *The Australian*

Pat Campbell, *The Canberra Times*

Eric Löbbecke, *The Australian*

'Budget 2017 was an overwhelming victory for the Australian Labor Party and the broader labour movement ... it was the budget of ideological surrender.'

— Anthony Albanese

'The Libs have ... chosen instead to become a pale red imitation of the Labor Party.'

— Cory Bernardi

'We are part of the world's weak-government club because the government of the day, if it's a centre-right government, cannot get its first-choice legislation through the parliament.'

— Tony Abbott

Mark Knight, *Herald Sun*

David Pope, *The Canberra Times*

Reg Lynch, *The Sun Herald*

Andrew Dyson, *The Age*

Cathy Wilcox, *The Sun-Herald*

'They're corporatist, globalist media who are adamantly opposed to an economic nationalist agenda like Donald Trump has ... If you think they are going to give you your country back without a fight, you are sadly mistaken. Every day it is going to be a fight.'
— Steve Bannon

'The public doesn't believe you people anymore.'
— Donald Trump

'I disagreed with George Bush all the time — never called him a pathological liar, because he was not. Just a conservative president. But this guy lies all of the time.'
— Bernie Sanders

'He never believed in anything except Charlie Kane. He never had a conviction except Charlie Kane in his life.'
— Citizen Kane

Pat Campbell, *The Canberra Times*

'The fake media is trying to silence us, but we will not let them. The people know the truth. The fake media tried to stop us from going to the White House, but I'm president and they're not.'
— Donald Trump

'We've been telling you for months the "destroy Trump" media will do anything in their power to take down this president ... Time after time, the professional Trump-haters over at the Clinton News Network, they've been proving my point.'
— Sean Hannity, Fox News

'Increasingly, I feel the creep of dread and sadness. Dread at a sense that no one knows, least of all, I fear, Mr. Trump, where this all may lead. And sadness that this spectacle is now the norm of the United States.'
— Dan Rather

'We don't want other countries and other leaders laughing at us anymore.'
— Donald Trump

First Dog on the Moon, *The Guardian*

Jon Kudelka, *The Australian*

'The Paris climate accord is simply the latest example of Washington entering into an agreement that disadvantages the United States, to the exclusive benefit of other countries, leaving American workers, who I love, and taxpayers to absorb the cost in terms of lost jobs, lower wages, shuttered factories, and vastly diminished economic production.'

— Donald Trump

'I applaud President Trump and his administration for dealing yet another significant blow to the Obama administration's assault on domestic energy production and jobs.'

— Senator Mitch McConnell

'Make our planet great again.'

— Emmanuel Macron

'I was elected to represent the citizens of Pittsburgh, not Paris.'

— Donald Trump

Alan Moir, *The Sydney Morning Herald*

David Pope, *The Canberra Times*

Mark Knight, *Herald Sun*

'The times in which we could completely depend on others are on the way out. I've experienced that in the last few days. We must really take our destiny into our own hands ... we must fight for our own future and our fate ourselves as Europeans.'

— Angela Merkel

'The fact that our friend and ally has come to question the very worth of its mantle of global leadership puts into sharper focus the need for the rest of us to set our own clear and sovereign course. To say this is not controversial. It is fact.'

— Chrystia Freeland, Canadian foreign affairs minister

'I have had the best reviews on foreign land. So I go to Poland and make a speech. Enemies of mine in the media, enemies of mine, are saying it was the greatest speech ever made on foreign soil by a president.'

— Donald Trump

Ron Tandberg, *The Age*

Ron Tandberg, *The Age*

Geoff Pryor, *The Saturday Paper*

'I've said it very simply. I think it could very well have been Russia. I think it could well have been other countries. I won't be specific. But I think a lot of people interfere ... Nobody really knows. Nobody really knows for sure.'
— Donald Trump

'President Trump said that he had heard the clear statements from President Putin about this being untrue, that the Russian leadership did not interfere in the election, and that he accepts these statements.'
— Sergey Lavrov, Russian foreign minister

'There was a very clear positive chemistry between the two ... There was not a lot of relitigating things from the past.'
— Rex Tillerson

Cathy Wilcox, *The Sun-Herald*

Greg Smith, *The Sunday Times*

Christopher Downes, *The Mercury*

Paul Zanetti, *www.zanetti.net.au*

Greg Smith, *The Sunday Times*

'My handshake with him — it wasn't innocent. It's not the be-all and the end-all of a policy, but it was a moment of truth.'
— Emmanuel Macron

'I mean, really. He's a very good person. And a tough guy, but look, he has to be. I think he is going to be a terrific president of France. But he does love holding my hand.'
— Donald Trump

'She's in such good physical shape ... beautiful.'
— Donald Trump on Brigitte Macron

'It's a rather interesting comment to make. I wonder if she could say the same of him?'
— Julie Bishop

Reg Lynch, *The Sun-Herald*

'The next election won't be won by drawing closer to Labor. The next election can only be won by drawing up new battlelines that give our people something to fight for; and the public something to hope for.'
— Tony Abbott

'For men with really small minds, for little men with soft, soft backbones, with no ticker, no heart, and no soul. That's who is running the Liberal Party now.'
— Peta Credlin

'I was going to say I've known him for a million years — it may feel like a million years — it's about 40 years.'
— Malcolm Turnbull

Jon Kudelka, *The Australian*

Sean Leahy, *The Courier Mail*

David Rowe, *Australian Financial Review*

'In 1944, Menzies went to great pains not to call his new political party, consolidating the centre-right of Australian politics, conservative, but rather the Liberal Party, which he firmly anchored in the centre of Australian politics ... The sensible centre was the place to be. It remains the place to be.'
— Malcolm Turnbull

'I'm sure that [Menzies] would very much approve of the notion that his party has been, and continues to be a broad church ... It's the party of John Stuart Mill and Edmund Burke, it's a coalition of classical liberals and conservatives and while ever it remains so, its best days can lay ahead of it.'
— John Howard

'I'm in no hurry to leave public life because we need strong Liberal conservative voices now, more than ever.'
— Tony Abbott

Cathy Wilcox, *The Sun-Herald*

Lindsay Foyle, *New Matilda*

Eric Löbbecke, *The Australian*

'Menzies said at the time: "We took the name 'Liberal' because we were determined to be a progressive party, willing to make experiments, in no sense reactionary but believing in the individual, his right and his enterprise, and rejecting the socialist panacea".'

— Malcolm Turnbull

'What it's sent is a very strong message to conservatives in Australia — you're no longer welcome within the party of Menzies. And I suspect if Sir Robert Menzies was alive today he would be considering an alternative.'

— Senator Cory Bernardi

Peter Broelman, *www.broelman.com.au*

Paul Zanetti, *www.zanetti.net.au*

Mark Knight, *Herald Sun*

'The reforms I am announcing today will entrench the co-operation between the agencies ... Importantly, ASIO, AFP, and Australian Border Force will all report directly to the Home Affairs Minister. This will ensure that these three important agencies have direct reporting into the cabinet.'

— Malcolm Turnbull

'Having made the promise to stop the boats and to make sure that we can keep our borders secure, we make this announcement today with this promise: the Home Affairs portfolio is dedicated to keeping Australians safe, to doing everything that we can to defeat the scourge of terrorism ... to work with our agencies in relation to transnational crime ... organised crime ... and other aspects of criminal activity within our country.'

— Peter Dutton

'I'd like to be convinced this is about national security, not Malcolm Turnbull's job security.'

— Bill Shorten

David Pope, *The Canberra Times*

Jon Kudelka, *The Australian*

David Rowe, *Australian Financial Review*

'The advice back then was that we didn't need the kind of massive bureaucratic change that the prime minister has in mind. I can only assume the advice has changed since then and no doubt the prime minister will give us more information in due course.'
— Tony Abbott

'I don't think this is a captain's call, I think this is Peter Dutton's call. I'm very concerned that these proposals aren't being pushed by our security agencies, they're being pushed by Peter Dutton.'
— Bill Shorten

'It's not about politics. It's about safety, Australians' public safety.'
— Malcolm Turnbull

Cathy Wilcox, *The Sun-Herald*

Fiona Katauskas, *Eureka Street*

Glen Le Lievre, *The Sun-Herald*

'We must avoid a media verdict, a verdict based on gossip. It's in the hands of the justice system, and one cannot judge before the justice system. After the justice system speaks, I will speak.'
— Pope Francis

'These matters have been under investigation now for two years. There have been leaks to the media. There has been relentless character assassination ... and for more than a month, claims that a decision on whether to lay charges was imminent. I'm looking forward, finally, to having my day in court. I'm innocent of these charges. They are false.'
— Cardinal George Pell

'You know the survivors have felt like this is a David and Goliath struggle, you've got individual people that are struggling — it's a momentous day for them.'
— Andrew Collins, abuse survivor

Ron Tandberg, *The Age*

Peter Broelman, *www.broelman.com.au*

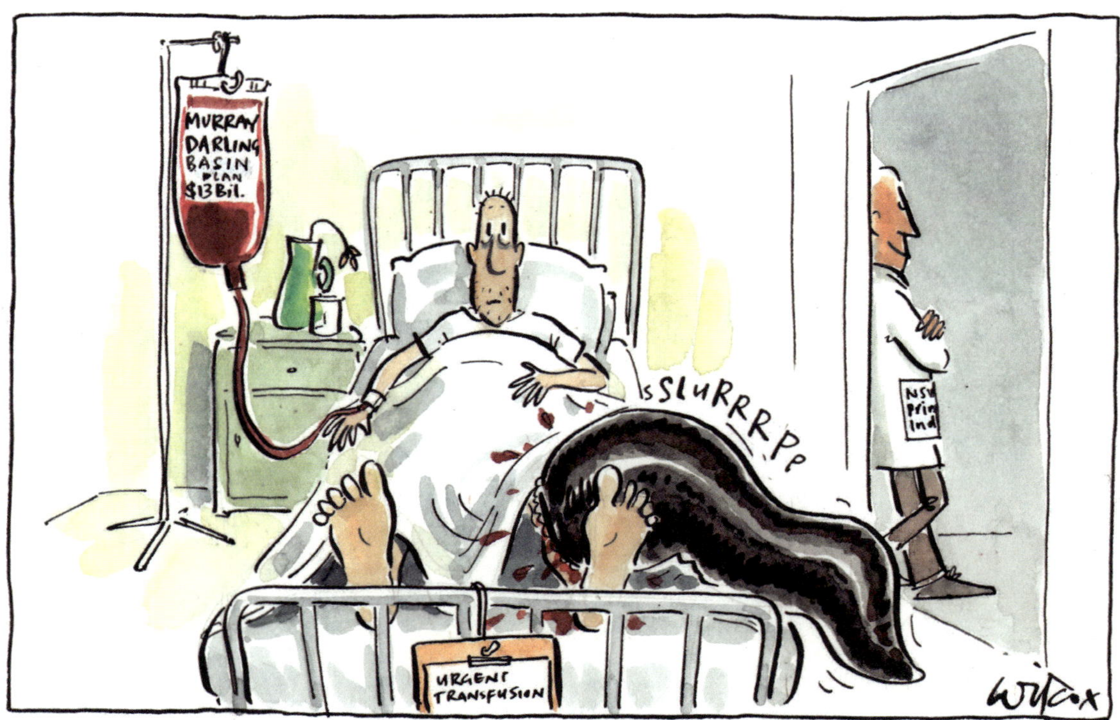

Cathy Wilcox, *The Sun-Herald*

'We have taken water, put it back into agriculture, so we could look after you and make sure we don't have the greenies running the show basically sending you out the back door, and that was a hard ask.'
— Barnaby Joyce

'He is absolutely incapable of doing the job he has been given.'
— Ian Hunter, South Australian water minister

'Suspected money laundering was conducted through CommBank accounts by way of cash deposits, many through IDMs, followed immediately by international and domestic transfers.'
— Australian Transaction Reports and Analysis Centre

'There has been an almost contemptuous disregard of the law … If you want to have a cultural shift in financial institutions … there is nothing like a jail term for their chief executive and board of directors to sharpen their thinking.'
— Nick Xenophon

Jon Kudelka, *The Australian*

Jon Kudelka, *The Australian*

David Rowe, *Australian Financial Review*

'The Crown prosecutor of Russia ... offered to provide the Trump campaign with some official documents and information that would incriminate Hillary and her dealings with Russia and be very useful to your father ... This is obviously very high level and sensitive information but is part of Russia and its government's support for Mr Trump ... What do you think is the best way to handle this information and would you be able to speak to Emin about it directly? I can also send this info to your father via Rhona, but it is ultra sensitive so wanted to send to you first.'

— Rob Goldstone email to Donald Trump Jr

'If it's what you say I love it especially later in the summer.'

— Donald Trump Jr

'This is the greatest Witch Hunt in political history. Sad!'

— Donald Trump

Andrew Dyson, *The Age*

Alan Moir, *The Sydney Morning Herald*

Alan Moir, *The Sydney Morning Herald*

David Rowe, *Australian Financial Review*

Geoff Pryor, *The Saturday Paper*

'This is Nixonian. Deputy Attorney General Rod Rosenstein must immediately appoint a special counsel to continue the Trump/Russia investigation ... this investigation must be independent and thorough in order to uphold our nation's system of justice.'

— Bob Casey

'This is a centipede. I guarantee you there will be more shoes to drop, I can just guarantee it.'

— John McCain

'I did not collude, nor know of anyone else in the campaign who colluded, with any foreign government ... I had no improper contacts. I have not relied on Russian funds to finance my business activities in the private sector.'

— Jared Kushner

Mark Knight, *Herald Sun*

'We are taking a stand … the staggering number of leaks undermining the ability of our government to protect this country.'

— Jeff Sessions

'I'll get to the person who leaked that to you. … Reince Priebus — if you want to leak something — he'll be asked to resign very shortly. Reince is a fucking paranoid schizophrenic, a paranoiac.'

— Anthony Scaramucci

'Look at the way I have been treated lately, especially by the media. No politician in history, and I say this with great surety, has been treated worse or more unfairly. You can't let them get you down, you can't let the critics and the naysayers get in the way of your dreams.'

— Donald Trump

Ron Tandberg, *The Age*

Matt Golding, *The Sunday Age*

Andrew Dyson, *The Age*

'Sean's doing a good job, excellent job.'
— Donald Trump

'The fish stinks from the head down. But I can tell you two fish that don't stink, ok, and that's me and the president ... There are people inside the administration that think it is their job to save America from this president. That is not their job ... to rein him in or slow down his agenda ... The swamp will not defeat him.'
— Anthony Scaramucci

'The Trump presidency that we fought for, and won, is over ... I feel jacked up. Now I'm free. I've got my hands back on my weapons ... I am definitely going to crush the opposition. There's no doubt ... I built a fucking machine at Breitbart ... And now I'm about to go back, knowing what I know, and we're about to rev that machine up. And rev it up we will do.'
— Steve Bannon

David Rowe, *Australian Financial Review*

Mark Knight, *Herald Sun*

David Rowe, *Australian Financial Review*

'North Korea best not make any more threats to the United States. They will be met with fire and fury like the world has never seen.'

— Donald Trump

'We are not just the superpower. We were a superpower, we are now a hyper-power. Nobody in the world, especially not North Korea, comes close to challenging our military capabilities.'

— Sebastian Gorka, US ambassador to the UN

'We are joined at the hip. The American alliance is the bedrock of our national security.'

— Malcolm Turnbull

'Countries like Australia that join the military adventure against the DPRK, blindly following the US, will never avoid the counter-measures of justice by the DPRK.'

— North Korean Ministry of Foreign Affairs

Mark Knight, *Herald Sun*

David Rowe, *Australian Financial Review*

Judy Horacek, *The Age*

'America was, until this last generation, a white country designed for ourselves and our posterity. It is our creation, it is our inheritance, and it belongs to us ... a race that travels forever on an upward path. To be white is to be a creator, an explorer, a conqueror.'

— Richard B. Spencer

'When and if fascism comes to America it will not be labelled *made in Germany*; it will not be marked with a swastika; it will not even be called fascism; it will be called, of course, *Americanism*.'

— *New York Times* reporter, 1938

Sean Leahy, *The Courier Mail*

David Pope, *The Canberra Times*

Matt Golding, *The Sunday Age*

'If you're not outraged, you're not paying attention.'
— Heather Heyer, murdered at Charlottesville

'We condemn in the strongest possible terms this egregious display of hatred, bigotry, and violence on many sides. On many sides.'
— Donald Trump

'The longer they talk about identity politics, I got 'em. I want them to talk about racism every day. If the left is focused on race and identity, and we go with economic nationalism, we can crush the Democrats.'
— Steve Bannon

'If Senator Hanson wanted to prove it is possible for dangerous extremists to get into the Senate chambers, she proved it all right. She proved Australians have something to fear — and it is her.'
— Jacqui Lambie

Peter Broelman, *www.broelman.com.au*

Mark Knight, *Herald Sun*

Matt Golding, *The Sunday Age*

'Malcolm Turnbull was the communications minister and now he's the prime minister ... Now there was a time when people said it wouldn't happen, but George and I kept the faith. We voted for Malcolm Turnbull in every ballot he's ever been in ... We have to deliver a couple of things, and one of those we've got to deliver before too long is marriage equality ... we're going to get it. I think it might even be sooner than everyone thinks. And your friends in Canberra are working on that outcome.'

— Christopher Pyne

'If he's to be believed on Friday night, that loyalty was never there, which is incredibly disappointing. This is one of the reasons why the public turn off politicians, because we don't tell them what we think. And it looks like one of our number has been caught out ... You've got to be fair dinkum with the Australian people, and it looks like that's not been true of Christopher.'

— Tony Abbott

John Farmer, *The Mercury*

"IT'LL BLOW OVER."

Glen Le Lievre, *Crikey*

Glen Le Lievre, *The Sun-Herald*

David Pope, *The Canberra Times*

Dean Alston, *The West Australian*

'I am disappointed that Qantas has become an active promoter for same-sex marriage ... Your statement leaves me no option but to use other airlines where possible for my extensive travelling.'

— Margaret Court

'Qantas speaks out on a number of social issues from Indigenous recognition to gender diversity and marriage equality. We do so because we believe these issues are about the fundamental Australian value of fairness and we're the national carrier.'

— Qantas spokesperson

'Don't use an iconic brand and the might of a multi-billion-dollar business on issues best left to the judgements of individuals and elected decision-makers. I'd prefer publicly listed companies stick to their knitting and that is delivering the services for their customers and providing a return for their shareholders.'

— Peter Dutton

Cathy Wilcox, *The Sun-Herald*

'The Australian Christian lobby described our children as the stolen generation. We love our children. And I object, as do every person who cares about children, and as do all those couples in this country, same-sex couples who have kids, to be told our children are a stolen generation. You talk about unifying moments? It is not a unifying moment. It is exposing our children to that kind of hatred.'

— Penny Wong

'You can't have a parliamentary election they'll be saying next because ... someone will say something outrageous and unfair and cruel and wrong about a candidate.'

— Malcolm Turnbull

'If you don't like same-sex marriage, vote no. If you're worried about religious freedom and freedom of speech, vote no, and if you don't like political correctness, vote no, because voting no will help to stop political correctness in its tracks.'

— Tony Abbott

Pat Campbell, *The Canberra Times*

Sean Leahy, *The Courier Mail*

Cathy Wilcox, *The Sun-Herald*

Cathy Wilcox, *The Sun-Herald*

David Pope, *The Canberra Times*

'Strong leaders carry out their promises. Weak leaders break them. I'm a strong leader.'
— Malcolm Turnbull

'Strong leaders do not need to say, "I am a strong leader". They prove it with their actions.'
— Bill Shorten

'These postal ballots and a plebiscite are never actually binding — legally they cannot be binding.'
— Eric Abetz

'The voluntary postal voting method ... is likely to ensure that not only will a minority of Australians vote, but also that large sections of the community will be disfranchised.'
— Malcolm Turnbull, 1997

'My friend Malcolm Turnbull was much better in those days.'
— Justice Michael Kirby

David Pope, *The Canberra Times*

'Because of 70-year-old Canadian laws I had been a dual citizen from birth, and that Canadian law changed a week after I was born and required me to have actively renounced Canadian citizenship.'
— Larissa Waters

'It is pretty amazing, isn't it, that you have had two out of nine Greens Senators didn't realise they were citizens of another country ... It shows incredible sloppiness on their part.'
— Malcolm Turnbull

'One Nation can confirm none of its senators have dual citizenships.'
— Pauline Hanson

'He is choosing to believe that he was never British ... He is preferring to believe that he was never British because he has no allegiance or exercised any citizenship arrangement.'
— Malcolm Roberts spokesperson

Dean Alston, *The West Australian*

David Pope, *The Canberra Times*

Andrew Dyson, *The Age*

'You know, when you nominate for parliament, there is actually a question — you have got to address that Section 44 question, and you've got to tick the box and confirm that you are not a citizen of another country.'

— Malcolm Turnbull

'In 2006, my mother lodged documents with the Italian consulate in Brisbane to become an Italian citizen. In doing so, it would appear that she made an application for me to become an Italian citizen as well. I was 25 years old at the time.'

— Matt Canavan

'I've never seen a parliament like this one — we're a year into it, and we're still working out who's allowed in and who's not.'

— Tony Burke

Pat Campbell, *The Canberra Times*

David Rowe, *Australian Financial Review*

David Rowe, *Australian Financial Review*

Journalist: Have you gone back and triple, quadruple-checked your own background there?
Barnaby Joyce: Everyone has had the conversation with their mothers and fathers ... When I was asleep, did you make me a citizen of Botswana? I am an Australian – no problems there.'

'The deputy prime minister, who I suppose we should now call the foreign minister or the leader of the "dual Nationals'"is, unwittingly or not, a dual citizen.'

– Bill Shorten

'Bill Shorten has sought to use a foreign political party to raise serious allegations in a foreign parliament, designed to undermine confidence in the Australian government.'

– Julie Bishop

David Pope, *The Canberra Times*

David Pope, *The Canberra Times*

Geoff Pryor, *The Saturday Paper*

Malcolm Turnbull: Well, I'm not going to comment on the gentleman you describe, you've referred to, but let me just say this about the budget: the budget was a great success.
Journalist: Will Tony Abbott ever feature in a Turnbull cabinet?
Malcolm Turnbull: Look, again, I know you're interested in the gentleman you describe, but I'm not.
Journalist: You keep using that phrase ... you don't want to say his name?
Malcolm Turnbull: No, no, no, listen, look, please ...

'Tony Abbott has to ask one simple question – his constant critiquing of the government, who's benefiting most? Who's most encouraged by those comments? Is it the party members who want to see a continuation of the Liberal government? The answer is no. Is it my parliamentary colleagues who want to see them retain their own seats and the Government stay in office? The answer is no.'
– Josh Frydenberg

Alan Moir, *The Sydney Morning Herald*

Andrew Dyson, *The Age*

Geoff Pryor, *The Saturday Paper*